Contents

 Fiction

Witnesses
page 2

Play

Gone Too Far
page 22

 Non-fiction

Forensics
page 30

Written by
Penny Kendal

Illustrated by
Daniel Tarrant

Series editor **Dee Reid**

ALWAYS LEARNING

PEARSON

Before reading Witnesses

Characters

Liam

Jen

The boys

New vocabulary

ch1 p4	avoid	
ch2 p8	doubled back	
ch2 p11	derelict	
ch3 p15	sneered	
ch4 p17	cousin	
ch4 p20	unusual	
ch4 p20	ruined	

Introduction

Liam and Jen were walking home through the park when they heard a scream. In a clearing a short distance away, they saw a group of boys kicking someone on the ground. Jen wanted to call the police but Liam stopped her. He had seen something that made him decide he could not call the police.

Witnesses

Chapter One

It was getting dark as Liam and Jen walked through the park. It had been raining and there were patches of mud on the grass.

"Nice trainers!" said Liam as he put his arm around Jen.

"Thanks," said Jen. "My dad bought them for me in London. I don't want to get them muddy so we'll have to stay on the path."

Jen leaned over to kiss Liam. Then they heard a scream. Liam charged through the trees to see what was going on. There was another scream. Jen followed him, trying to avoid the mud on the grass. Then they both stopped and stared.

In a clearing, a short distance away, they could see a group of four boys. They were kicking someone on the ground. The person on the ground was screaming in pain.

Jen heard a boy's voice. "Stop! We don't want to kill him."

But the others didn't stop, they carried on kicking.

Then the screaming stopped.

The same boy spoke again. "You've gone too far!"
Jen saw his blond hair as he bent down to the boy
on the ground. "He looks bad!"

"You were kicking him just as hard as us!" said a
dark-haired boy.

Jen grabbed Liam's hand. "We've got to call the
police," she whispered, "and an ambulance." She
pulled her mobile from her pocket.

Liam snatched it from her. "We can't. Just pretend
you didn't see anything."

Jen looked surprised. "What do you mean? That boy is badly hurt. We have to tell someone."

"I know one of them," said Liam quietly.

"I don't care," said Jen. "We have to call 999."

"No," argued Liam.

Jen pulled away. "Well if you're not going to get help, I am!" and she turned and ran.

Chapter Two

Jen ran across the grass towards a park gate
but it was already locked. She doubled back
through the trees. It was the fastest way to the
other gate. But suddenly the boys were all there,
only metres away.

She had got lost and come out close to the
clearing. She was in clear sight of the gang. She
ducked behind a tree but it was too late. The
blond boy had seen her.

"Hey you!" he called. "Come here!"

Jen was shaking with fear. The boy they had
attacked was lying still on the ground.

"She must have seen something," said the tallest
boy. "We'll have to make her keep quiet."

The tall boy raised his fists and came towards her.

"Leave it," said the blond one.

"She'll grass us up," said the tall one. "Do you want to go to prison?"

"Let's lock her up," said the dark-haired boy. "Then we can decide what to do. I know just the place."

Two boys grabbed her arms. They pulled her through a gap in a hedge and led her to a derelict house just outside the park.

"Please, let me go!" Jen begged.

"Shut up," said the blond boy and he pushed her inside an old shed in the garden and padlocked the door.

Chapter Three

Jen banged on the door. "Please! Let me out!"
Then she began to sob. If only she had her phone
but Liam had taken it when she was going to call
for help. Now she couldn't get help for the boy *or*
for herself.

After shouting and banging for ages Jen sat down. She looked at her new trainers. They were covered in mud.

Jen must have dozed off because she woke feeling cold and hungry. She banged on the door again and called at the top of her voice. Suddenly something made a noise outside. Had someone come to rescue her?

The door opened and Jen saw the boy with blond hair. She leapt at him, clawing his face with her long nails. The boy backed away. Jen got out of the shed but he caught hold of her arm. Then she broke free and ran.

But she ran straight into the dark-haired boy who grabbed her firmly. He was bigger and stronger than the blond boy.

"Going somewhere?" he sneered. He dragged her back to the shed. "Lucky I was here," the dark-haired boy told the blond boy. "We'll have to teach her a lesson."

Chapter Four

"Stay with her this time and make sure she doesn't try anything else," said the dark-haired boy. "I'll get Freddy."

Jen shivered. *What were they going to do to her?* Then she remembered that Liam had said he knew one of the gang. She didn't know which one but anything was worth a try.

"My boyfriend knows you," she said to the blond boy.

"Who's your boyfriend?" he asked.

"Liam Cooke," said Jen.

The boy's mouth dropped open. "Liam Cooke is your boyfriend?" he asked.

"Yes," said Jen. "How do you know him?"

"He's my cousin," the boy replied.

Jen gasped. No wonder Liam had wanted to keep quiet.

"I'll help you escape," said the boy. "But you have to promise not to grass us up. If you do, you're dead."

"I'll keep quiet," said Jen. "I promise."

The boy held open the shed door.

"This is the police!" shouted a loud voice. "Come out with your hands up."

The police grabbed the boy and led him away in handcuffs.

"Jen!" someone called. It was Liam!

"I'm so sorry," he said, hugging her.

"You called the police?" she asked.

"Yes," said Liam.

"But how did you find me?" asked Jen.

"When your mum called and said you hadn't come home I rang the police and told them everything," said Liam. "The boy is in hospital but he'll be OK. You were right. We should have phoned them straight away. I came back to help look for you and saw an unusual trainer print in the mud. I showed the police. We followed your footprints and they led here. It's lucky you were wearing your new trainers." Jen looked down at her dirty, ruined trainers. "Yeah, sort of," she said.

Quiz

Literal comprehension

p4 Why does Jen want to stay on the path?

p14 What does Jen do when the blond-haired boy comes into the shed?

p20 How did Liam help the police to find Jen?

Inferential comprehension

p13 Who does Jen think has made the noise outside?

p17 Why is it a good idea to tell the boy that Liam knows him?

p20 Why does Jen say "Yeah, sort of," at the end of the story?

Personal response

• Would you have called the police if you were Liam?

• How would you feel if you were locked in a shed without your mobile?

• How do you think Liam feels when he learns that Jen is not at home?

Author's style

p13 What phrase does the author use to explain that Jen shouted loudly?

p15 What words does the dark-haired boy use to scare Jen?

p16 What is the effect of using a question in the second paragraph?

21

Characters

- **Leo** (Liam's cousin)
- **Dan**
- **Freddy** (the gang leader)
- **Rick**

Setting the scene

Rick has told the gang that a boy stole his money, so the gang wait until the boy is walking through the park and then they attack him. As far as they are concerned the boy deserves all he gets.

Leo: You've gone too far! He looks bad!

Dan: You were kicking him just as hard as us!

Freddy: He deserves it. He took Rick's money.

Rick: Yeah! Like I told you, he took the money from my pocket and ran off.

Freddy: No one does that to one of the gang and gets away with it.

Dan: He's a thief! Everyone knows that.

Rick: Yeah, a nasty little thief. That's why I called you to help me sort him out. He deserves everything he got.

Leo: Well get your money off him then!

Freddy: Go on, Rick. Get your money back.

Dan: Why are you just standing there, Rick? It's your money.

Rick: He's not going anywhere. I'll get it in a minute.

Leo: I'll get it, shall I?

Freddy: Go on then.

Leo: There's nothing in this pocket.

Dan: Try the other pocket.

Leo: There's nothing there.

Dan: Try the back pockets.

Leo: Nothing.

Rick: He must have chucked the money as we were chasing him.

Leo: If he'd done that we would have seen it.

Dan: Where's the money, Rick?

Leo: And why didn't you want to look in his pockets?

Rick: No reason.

Freddy: What's going on, Rick?

Leo: He didn't take your money, did he? You lied to us!

Freddy: That's rubbish. Rick wouldn't lie to us!

Rick: He deserves everything he got. I promise you that.

Freddy: But did he take your money?

Rick: Well, no. But he is a thief! He took my place on the team! He's useless at football and he got me kicked off the team!

Leo: I told you Rick made this all up!

Freddy: You shouldn't have lied to us, Rick.

Dan: You should have told us the truth. We could have made him turn down the place on the team.

Leo: We didn't have to beat him up.

Rick: Well it's done now. He won't be playing football for a while.

Leo: He might be dead!

Rick: He's not dead. He just looks bad.

Leo: He needs to go to hospital.

Dan: We can't call an ambulance. The police will be on to us.

Freddy: Listen all of you. Not a word to anyone and no 999 calls. Got that?

Leo: But...

Freddy: Pretend you weren't here. You did nothing. You saw nothing.

Dan: Yeah and don't worry about him, someone will find him.

Rick: Come on, why are we hanging around? Let's get out of here.

Dan: Hang on! There's someone over there!

Leo: Hey you! Come here!

Freddy: She must have seen something. We'll have to make her keep quiet.

Leo: Haven't we done enough?

Freddy: She'll grass us up. Do you want to go to prison?

Rick: I don't want to go to prison!

Freddy: We can't hang about here.

Dan: Let's lock her up. Then we can decide what to do. I know just the place.

Freddy: And Rick – you're out of the gang.

Quiz

Text comprehension

p23 Why does Freddy get the gang to attack the boy?
p24 Why is Rick reluctant to search the boy's pockets?
p28 Why do the gang think they have to do something about Jen?

Vocabulary

p24 Find a word meaning 'thrown away'.
p26 Find a word meaning 'unskilful'.
p28 Find a phrase meaning 'inform the police'.

Before reading FORENSICS

Find out about

- how police use evidence from shoeprints, insects
  and DNA to track down criminals.

New vocabulary

p31 scientists

p31 evidence

p33 wear and tear

p33 database

p34 a suspect

p34 traced

p34 receipt

p38 identical

Introduction

Forensic scientists look at evidence to find clues to
solve crimes. Sometimes they can get evidence from a
shoeprint or from insects that are found near the body
which gives the scientists clues to the time of death.
They also use DNA to track down criminals.

FORENSICS

What is Forensics?

Forensics is the use of science to solve crimes.
Forensic scientists look at many types of evidence:
fingerprints, shoeprints, DNA, handwriting, teeth
and even insects. By looking at these things and
other pieces of evidence, forensic scientists can find
clues to help solve the crime.

POLICE LINE DO NOT CROSS

Evidence

Here are 3 different types of evidence used in forensics.

Shoeprints		Shoeprints can help to identify criminals.
Insects		Insects found on or around a body can help scientists work out a person's time of death.
DNA		DNA from one cell of skin or spot of blood can be used to identify a person.

Shoeprints

Many people wear the same brand of shoes but some things can change the shoeprint:

- the way the person walks

- wear and tear

- small stones and other rubbish picked up when walking.

There is a shoe database that forensic scientists use to solve crimes. There are more than 20,000 different shoeprints in the database.

A Shoeprint Case

In 2004, a woman was murdered in her home. Police had a suspect but needed evidence. A shoeprint in blood was found on the woman's floor. The shoe was identified using the shoeprint database. These shoes were made in 2002 for JJB Sports. Police then traced the shop where the actual pair of shoes were sold. They found the shop's copy of the receipt showing that the suspect had bought these shoes. This evidence helped to convict the suspect.

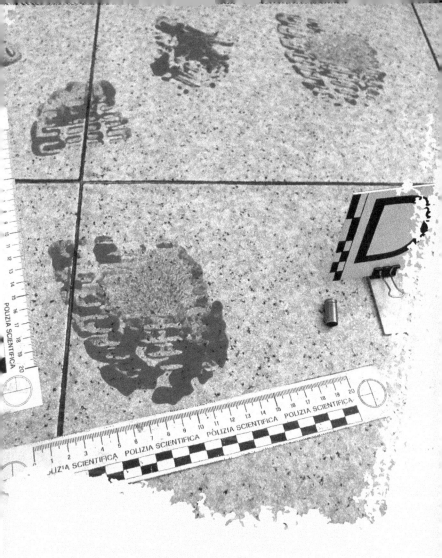

Shoeprints are not always good evidence.

One criminal stuck smaller soles on to his

shoes to confuse police!

Insects

When a body is found, police need to know the time of death. Insects in and around the body can give clues. Flies like to feed on dead bodies.

The life of a fly

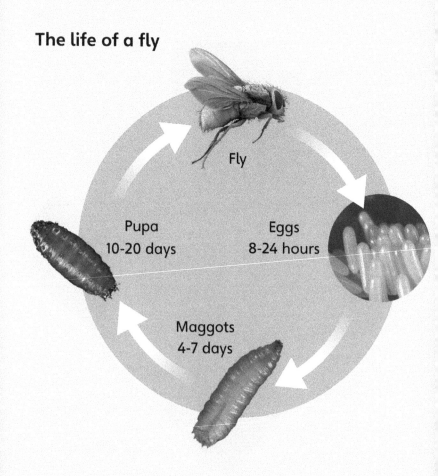

Fly

Pupa
10-20 days

Eggs
8-24 hours

Maggots
4-7 days

Scientists can use this information to work out the time of death. For example:

> A man's body is found.

> He was seen with a woman two weeks before. She is a suspect but police need to know when he died.

> The maggots on the body were at the pupa stage. So the man could have died the day he was seen with the woman.

> She is questioned and admits murder.

DNA

Every person's DNA is different unless they are an identical twin. DNA can be found in a hair or even a small piece of dandruff. So if the police find a trace of DNA at the scene of the crime they can link it to a suspect.

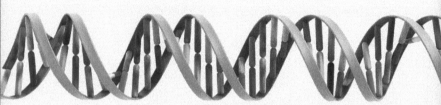

The first crime solved using DNA was the case of Colin Pitchfork in 1988. DNA evidence showed that he had murdered two girls even though another man had confessed to one of the murders!

Contamination

There can be problems with DNA evidence. For example, if you pick up one piece of evidence and then pick up another piece, you can transfer DNA from one thing to the other thing. This is called contamination. But every week more and more crimes from murders to burglaries are solved using DNA.

Quiz

Text comprehension

Literal comprehension
p34 How do the police use the shoeprint database?
p36–37 How can the police use insects to work out
    the time of death?
p38 Why is DNA useful to forensic scientists?

Inferential comprehension
p35 How might some criminals confuse the police?
p37 Why do you think the woman confessed to
    the murder?
p38 What mistake might a forensic scientist make
    with DNA evidence?

Personal response
p34 How do you think the man felt when the
    police showed him the receipt for his shoes?
p38 How do you think Colin Pitchfork felt when
    an innocent man confessed?
• Do you think the police are getting better at
    tracking down criminals? Why?

Non-fiction features

p32 Think of a heading for each column on the chart.
p36 Why is this diagram a good way to present the
    information?
p37 What organisational device is used here?
    How does it help explain the information?

Published by Pearson Education Limited, Edinburgh Gate, Harlow, Essex, CM20 2JE.

www.pearsonschoolsandfecolleges.co.uk

Text © Pearson Education Limited 2012

Edited by Ruth Emm
Designed by Tony Richardson and Siu Hang Wong
Original illustrations © Pearson Education Limited 2012
Illustrated by Daniel Tarrant
Cover design by Siu Hang Wong
Cover illustration © Pearson Education Limited 2012

The right of Penny Kendal to be identified as author of this work has been asserted by her in accordance with the Copyright, Designs and Patents Act 1988.

First published 2012

2023
18

British Library Cataloguing in Publication Data
A catalogue record for this book is available from the British Library

ISBN 978 0 435 07151 6

Printed and Bound in the UK

Acknowledgements
The author and publisher would like to thank the following individuals and organisations for permission to reproduce photographs:

(Key: b-bottom; c-centre; l-left; r-right; t-top)

Alamy Images: Mark Hope 34; Science Photo Library Ltd: Claude Naridsany & Marie Perennou 36l, 36r, 36b, Jim Varney 37, Mauro Fermariello 35, Steve Gschmeissner 1, 36t; Shutterstock. com: Alexander Vasilgev 32bl, 38, carl ballou 31b, GoodMood Photo 32-33, krasku 31t, PePi 32cl, PhotoHappiness 32tl

Cover images: Back: Science Photo Library Ltd: Mauro Fermariello

All other images © Pearson Education

Every effort has been made to contact copyright holders of material reproduced in this book. Any omissions will be rectified in subsequent printings if notice is given to the publishers.